il est à la limite de la poésie

Henri Chopin (*Fylkingen International Bulletin*)

etruscan books

24a Fore Street
Buckfastleigh
South Devonshire TQ11 0AA

ISBN 1 901538 27 3

kob bok

selected texts of
bob cobbing
1948-1999

selected by

bob cobbing & jennifer pike

etruscan books

1999

ENGLISH
VOICE
PRINT

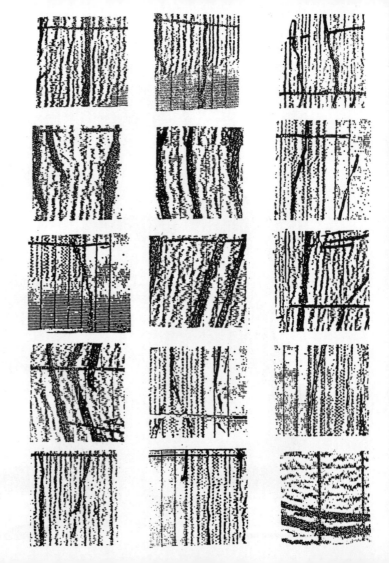

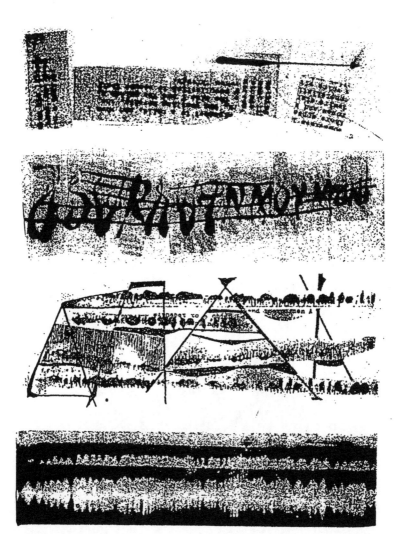

```
    a                              a
    a s                        s a
    a s i                    i s a
a                                 a
    a s i b              s    b i s a
a s                                s a
    a s i b i        o s    i b i s a
a s i                            i s a
      s i b i        b o s    i b i s
a s i b              s      b i s a
        i b i      a b o s    i b i
a s i b i            o s    i b i s a
        b i    s a b o s    i b
      s i b i        b o s    i b i s
          i    s a b o s    i
        i b i      a b o s    i b i
        b i    s a b o s    i b
        b i    s a b o s    i b
      i b i    s a b o      i b i
          i    s a b o s    i
      s i b i    s a b    i b i s
        b i    s a b o s    i b
    o s i b i    s a      i b i s o
        i b i    s a b o    i b i
    o s i b        s      b i s o
      s i b i    s a b    i b i s
    o s i                  i s o
  o s i b i    s a      i b i s o
    o s                        s o
  o s i b        s        b i s o
      o                          o
    o s i                  i s o

  o s                        s o
```

logico   logia   logico   logia
panzoo   minera   panzoo   icminera   panzoo
minera   logia   pan   zoo   era   logico   logia
zoo   logico   min   logia   panzoo
minera   panzoo   mineralog   era   minera
ne   era   ic   logi   co   era   zoo   pan   zoo   ic   pan   logial
pa   min   log   min   pan   logico   logic   zoo   era
logico   logia   min   pan   logia   pan   logico   zoo   pano
nera   co   pa   zoo   minera   logico   pan   zoo   logi
coni   logi   logico   panzoo   minera   logia
pan   logi   co   nin   lo   logia   logico   panzoo
zoo   era   gia   min   minera   zoo   pan
pan   log   zoologico   eralogia   logicomin
logico   minera   logia   panzoo   logico   icminera   logia   panzoo
panzoo   logico   logia   zoo   min   logia   panzoo   logic
minera   pan   era   logia   logico   logia
minera   panzoo   pan   mineralog   era   panzoo   logico
pan   logico   logico   era   logico   minera
pa   min   zoo   log   logi   min   minera   pan   pan   logia   zoo
no   era   la   zoo   era   co   era   logico   zoo   pan
log   loo   log   min   pan   logia   zoo   pano   logia
coni   log   logi   logico   pan   logia   panzoo   minera   pa
log   log   min   pan   minera   zoo   logico   pano   panzoo
nera   logi   minera   min   zoologico   logia   logico   pan
pan   pan   min   lo   logia   eralogi   locomin
logico   pan   logico   min   logico   zoo   pa
pan   log   pan   log   log   min   zoo   pa
pan   zoo   log   ico   min   era   log   min   ic   era   co   logico
zoo   log   ico   min   era   log   min   ic   era   co

KWATZ - in Chinese, He (pronounced Hay) - a meaningless word
like Vajrarāja's sacred sword, cutting the chain of thought

like a crouching golden-haired lion, to scare the deluded
like the noise made by a vibrating reed to probe deep into the

not a vocal shout but a kind of   enquirer's understanding
blast of awakening to reality

                                                    it deafened him for

                        three days

rinzai asked a disciple   whether striking with a stick   or exclaiming kwatz

                conveyed or awakened more truth

when the pupil answered neither, and on being further questioned

        exclaimed   kwatz   rinzai

                struck him with a stick

BIRD BEE

aasvogel   brolga   colibri   dickcissel

eyas   fauvette   gallinule   hagbolt

iiwi   jabiru   korora   lammergeyer

mallemuck   nelly   ossifrage   pickmaw

quelea   rotchie   shama   tinamou

umbrette   witwall   yoldring   zoozoo

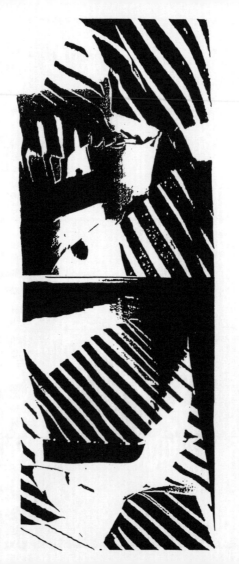

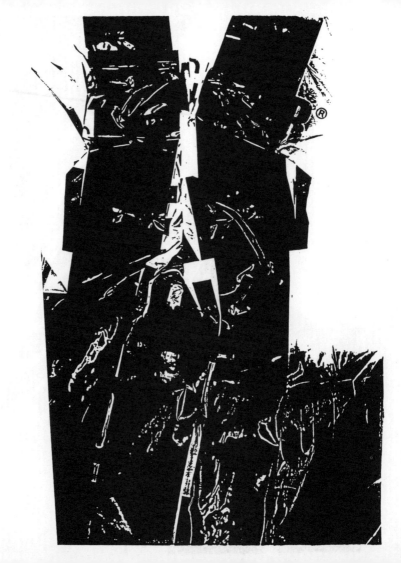

o furoba	basu
shokutaku	tēburu
shindai	beddo
tobira	doa
kamikiri	heakatto
o kashi	kēki
ame	kyandī
daidokoro	kicchin

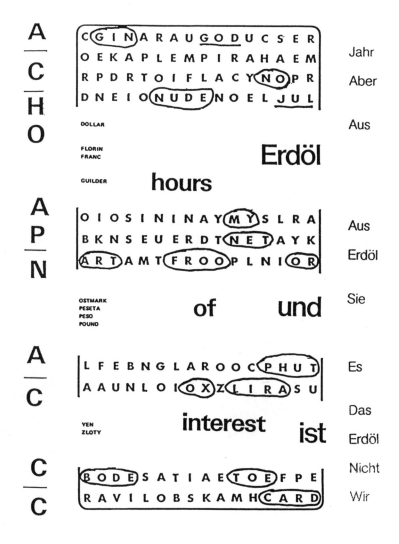

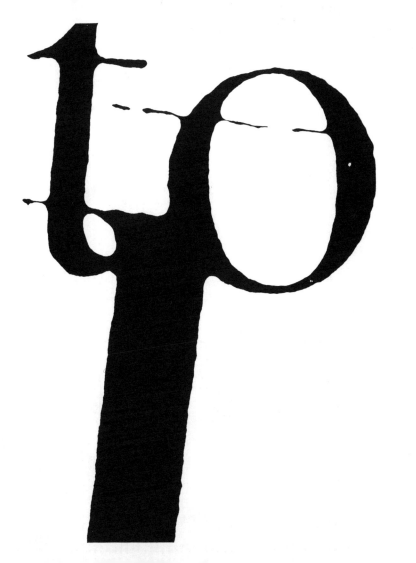

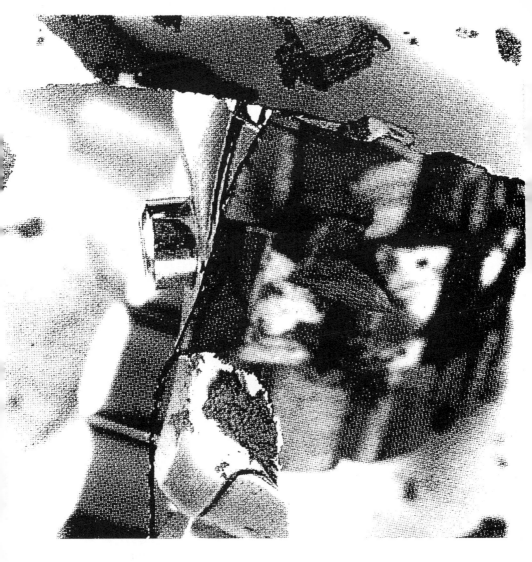

ninta
tara
tara ma ninta
tara ma tara
tara ma tara ma ninta
tara ma tara ma tara
tara ma tara ma tara ma ninta
tara ma tara ma tara ma tara
urapon
ukasar
ukasar urapon
ukasar ukasar
ukasar ukasar urapon
ukasar ukasar ukasar
xa
t'oa
'quo
t'oa t'oa
t'oa t'oa xa
t'oa t'oa t'oa
tokale
ahage
ahage tokale
ahage ahage
ahage ahage tokale
ahage ahage ahage

ping-pong

fiddle-faddle   pitter-patter

dribs and drabs   spic and span

riff-raff   mish-mash

flim-flam

chit-chat   tit-for-tat

knick-knack   zig-zag

sing-song   ding-dong

King Kong

criss-cross   shilly-shally

see-saw   hee-haw

flip-flop   hippity-hop

tick-tock   tic-tac-toe

eeny-meeny-miney-moe

bric-a-brac   clickety-clack

hickory-dickory-dock

kit and kaboodle

bibbety-bobbity-boo

razzle-dazzle   super-duper

helter-skelter   harum-scarum

hocus-pocus

willy-nilly   hully-gully

roly-poly   holy-moly

herky-jerky   walkie-talkie

namby-pamby   mumbo-jumbo

loosey-goosey   wing-ding

wham-bam   hob-nob

razza-matazz   rub-a-dub-dub

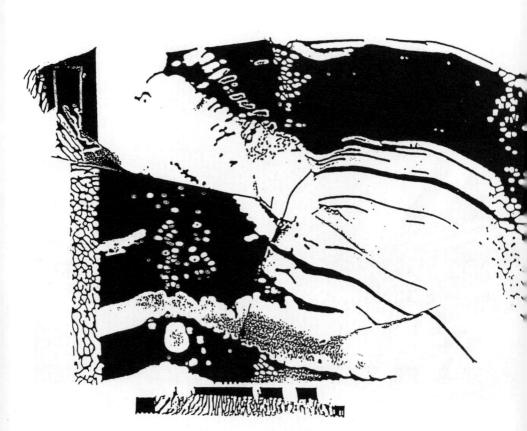

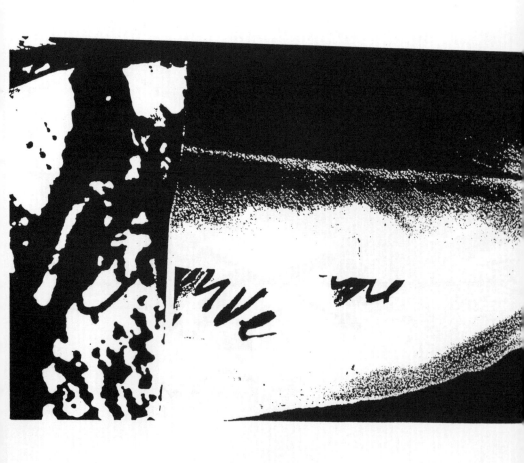

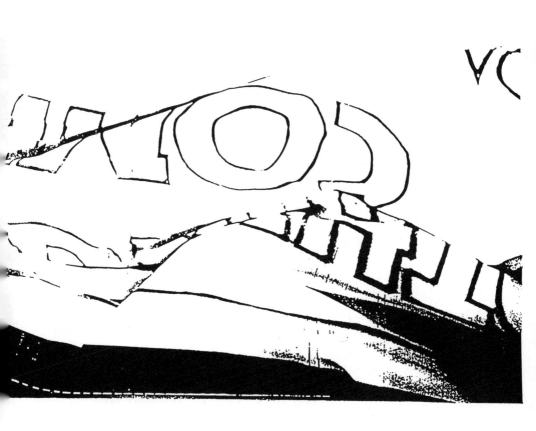

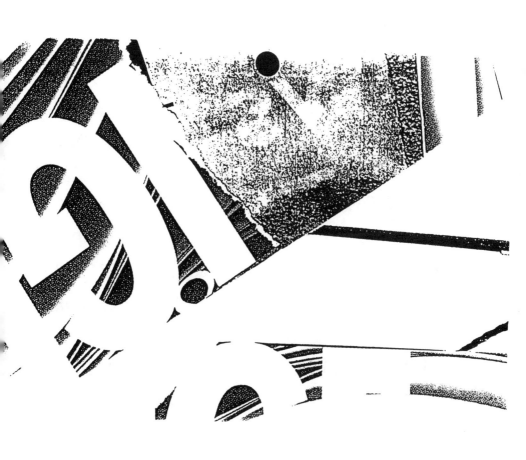

PETTIFOGGER	LARRIKIN
QUEER BLUFFER	SLAMTRASH
FUSTILUGS	SLOBBERER
PILGARLICK	SPALPEEN
SHOTTEN HERRING	GRANNY-JAZZER
SLUBBERDEGULLION	MOLLYFOCK
SLABBER	POPPA-LOPPER
TARLEATHER	KNUCKLEHEAD
SUMBITCH	PECKERWOOD
SLIVE-ANDREW	MOMSER
LUMMOCKS	POOPBUTT
SAPSKULL	SHITHEEL

LOBCOCK	MO MO
HODDY PEAK	GOOBER
BUFFLEHEAD	NUMBNUTTS
NIZZLE	DRONGO
FOPDOODLE	DINGBAT
NINNY-HAMMER	LOOGAN
NIMENOG	LUNKHEAD
NOODLE	DINGALING
SHANEY	HULVERHEAD
JUGGINS	ZIPALID
JOBBERNOWL	CUDDY
NODGECOCK	ISSACHAR

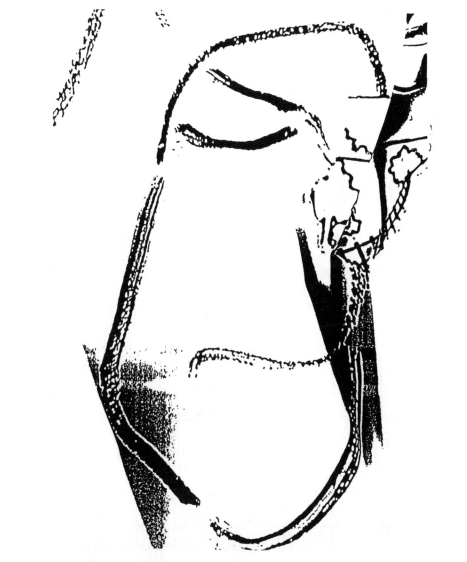

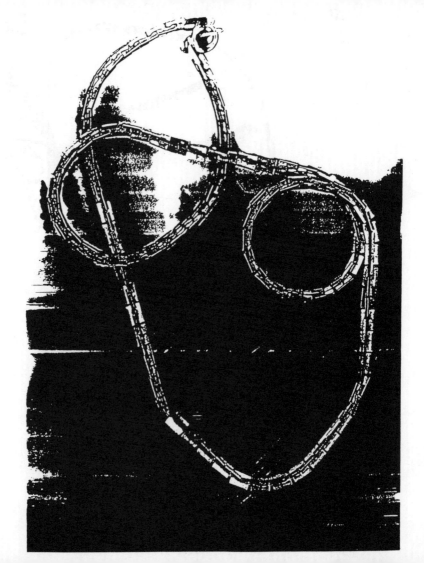

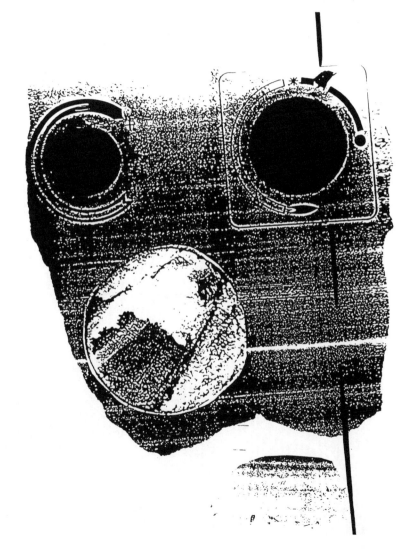

Predicting the weather
is one thing
predicting it correctly
is another
rain tends to fall
in irregular bursts
perhaps the invisible monster
theory isn't so daft
or the flapping of a
single butterfly's wings
clouds have no length-scale
water's the sensitive chaos
it isn't all as simple
as a snowflake
or thunder on a
hot and humid day
in just what sense
can the exact solution
to an approximated problem
be regarded as
the approximate solution
to an exact. exacting problem
when you can't begin
even to write it down
if it has the virtue
of simplicity
it has the vice.
of being wrong
if there really was
a theorem such as chaos
you keep the holes
and throw away the button
if the only animal in
existence was the elephant
then all those holes
in the skirting board
were made by tiny
elephants   fleas
have a natural length-scale
coastlines don't.

two for liz lochhead

a good fuck makes me feel like custard

a good feel makes me fuck like custard
good custard makes me feel like a fuck
fuck, like custard, makes me a good feel
makes 'fuck me' feel like a good custard
me, like custard, makes fuck a good feel
feel like me? custard makes a good fuck
like a good fuck, custard makes me feel
custard, like a fuck, makes me feel good

————————————————————

a good fuck makes me feel like custard

a good screw makes me feel like wet blancmange
a quick shag makes me feel like jelly
good sex makes me feel like a jam tart
intercourse makes me feel like stewed fruit
rock 'n roll makes me feel like rolypoly
a little lechery makes me feel like spotted dick
copulation makes me feel like apple crumble
intimacy makes me feel like gooseberry fool

ANAGRAMS   ARS MAGNA

DAEMONIC COMEDIAN
STARTLES STARLETS
STACCATO TOCCATOS
MISTUNE MINUETS
PEARLY PLAYER
ERRANT RANTER
CORONER CROONER
SINGER RESIGN
MERRIEST RIMESTER
HARMONIC CHOIRMAN
LILTS STILL
UMBRATED DRUMBEAT
PANTO ON TAP
SONIC ICONS
CHOPIN'S PHONICS
DRAB BARD
CROAT ACTOR
SCAT CATS
ROSIEST STORIES
COSMIC COMICS
EASTER TEASER
RISQUÉ QUIRES
PRINTER'S REPRINTS
STALE TALES

ALFRED FLARED
GERDA RAGED
GERALD GLARED
EDWIN WINED
DENNIS SINNED
ERNEST ENTERS
ELVIS LIVES
ZELDA LAZED
INANE ANNIE
WARNED ANDREW
ADVISE DAVIES
SAID SADI
RESENT ERNEST
BLAME MABEL
MOROSE ROMEOS
STERN ERNST
WARDEN ANDREW
INGRID RIDING
DENIS DINES
CATHY'S YACHTS
RYAN'S YARNS
VERA'S RAVES
VAGUEST GUSTAVE
GNAWED GWENDA
CANNY NANCY
AIMLESS MELISSA
SNIDE DENIS
RODNEY YONDER

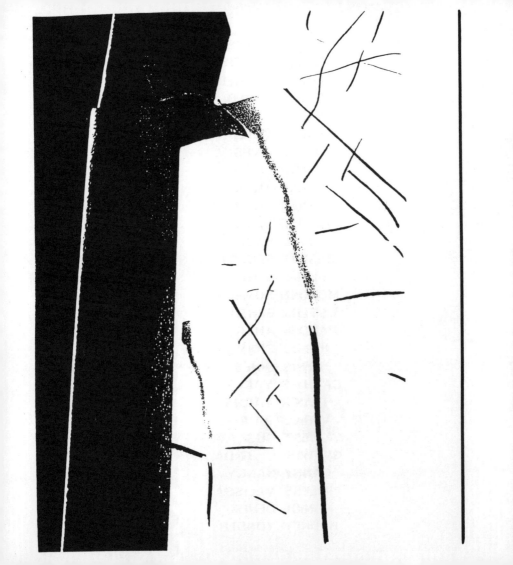

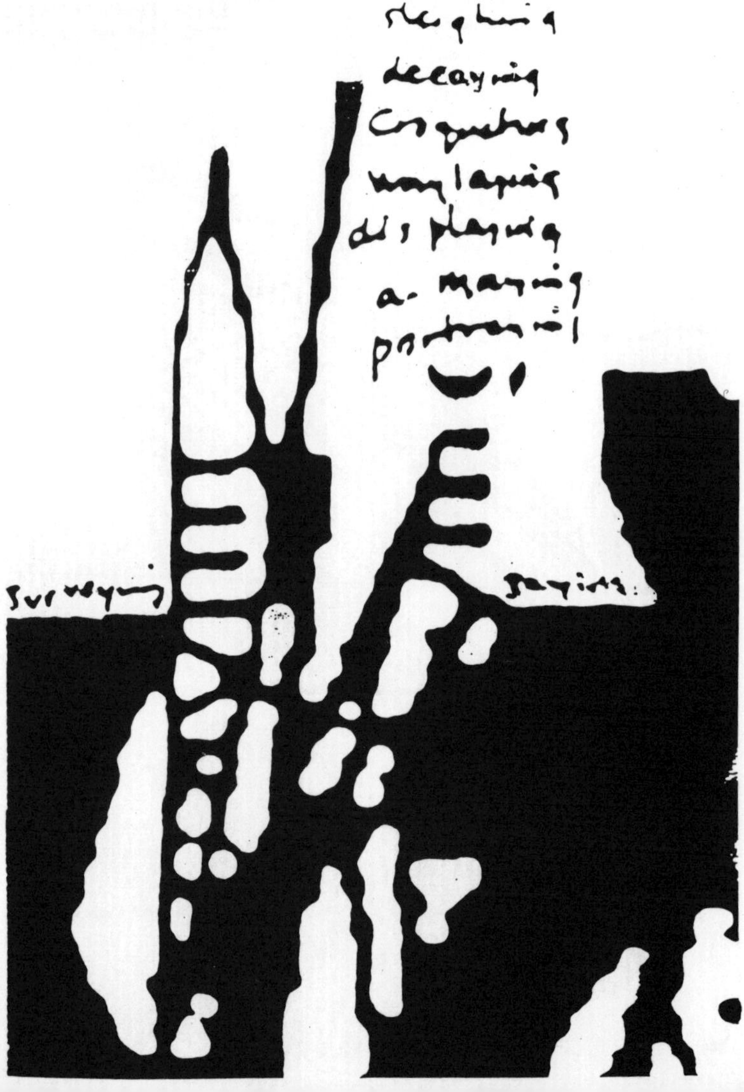
decaying
dis playing
a- mazing
Surveying
saying:

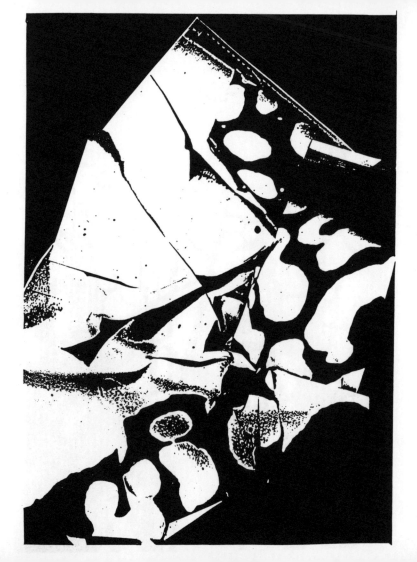

bather   breath

bertha   bakers

breather heart   breathe
bleeding   hea

breathe inn

bleeding heart   he
brabble   bestars

the   aching

                        ather
                        ding
her

tha   heart   athe

:hing   breathe

reak

e   breather   breathin

thing

r   breathe

a   bakers   brake

her heart   breathe in
ing heart   hearth

he inn

Ao	Bi	Bu
Ding	Dou sai	Ge si
Gu	Gui	Hu
Huang	Jian	Jiao dou
Jue	Kui	Li
Ling	Pai xiao	Pan
Pi	Xun	Yong
Yi	You	Zun
	Chi	Ying

I - ro   ha   ni - ho - he - to

Chi - ri - nu - ru   wo! Wa - ka

yo   ta - re   so   tsu - ne   na -

ra - mu? U - wi   no   o - ku -

ya - ma   Ke - fu   ko - ye - te

A - sa - ki   yu - me   mi - shi

We - hi   mo   se - su   N - nnn

aawaiTGcaqiic

aq‾bhkxajp ͨ i ͨ ɜ𝑥 ͨ 𝑏CHpA‾u

XqiiPhai‾imiagi iC=(_haaxe)

VƐQ!HpIhpap]Esiim ͨ i‾iixaiiri‾ciyic

ALrq!i𝑥0 ͨ b Fpt ͨ O ͨ !xIxfSA

ͨ hb ͨ gpxib} ͨ ͨ p ͨ (ͨ apɜ ͨ Ep ͨ A ͨ 6pi ͨͨ .)

hv ͨ xNxvaipyepaxi‾)yɜpb ͨͨ irppqh

dId!Apxpyp ispiqiic‾acc‾igiiciai

pp ͨͨ iAapxhxadi‾rh ͨ] ͨ ai ͨͨ b!Caf‾}

ͨ bxpQNAxx ApCI‾ ͨ E !AɜIY𝑥

axdihbip ͨ t‾qpbidAI cdct ͨ t}CI ͨ !

jrbOp}ph ͨ q ͨ tdox ͨ h0ip ͨ ‾j! ͨ qxiYEi

Ftttt ͨ A ͨ t!x}xi ze)BrjpBAjp

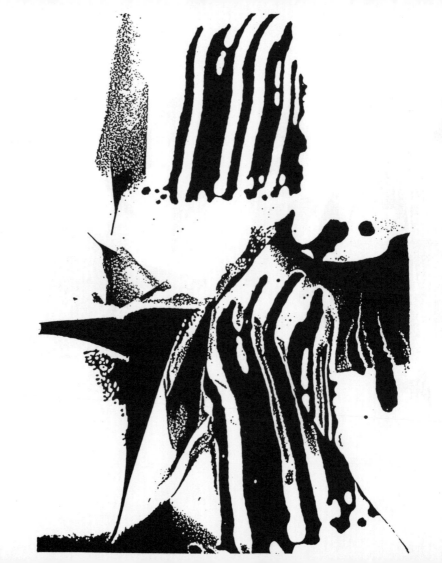

CONFUSIONS

i

SAC   is a medical & biological word
      not a dressmaker's or tailor's;
      see SAC(QUE)

SACHET, see French words

SACK,   dismiss(al)

SAC(QUE)   For the garment, SACK
      is the right form. The other
      spellings are pseudo-French,
      wrong in different degrees:
      there is no French word SACQUE;
      there is a French word SAC,
      but it is not, as the English
      SACK is or has been,
      the name for a particular
      garment

SARK,   a garment worn
     next to the skin

STARK,   see stark naked (from
      START naked) absolutely
      without clothes

STARK NAKED,   unadulterated
      spirit, esp. raw
      gin

ii

As the Scotch fir is
not a fir, strictly
speaking, but a pine
& as we shall continue
to ignore this fact, it
is plain that the matter concerns
the botanist more than the man
in the street.

Calalu
Malanga
Yauta
was as
Okra
Gumbo
Quimbombo

Potato
Kumara
Batata
like
Fra–Fra
Fura–Fura
Fabriama
Daso

Cassava
Manioc
Yuca
Sagu
then
Persimmon
Black Sapota
Kaki

Water Chestnut
(Trapa Natans)
Water Caltrop
Horse's Hooves
or
Ilama
Monkey Apple
Soncoya
Cherimoya
Bullock's Heart

Brionne
Chayote
Christophine
Choko
is
Xuxu
Pepinella
Cho–Cho

Ambarella
Golden Hog
Spondias
Yellow Mombin
Jungli Amba
with
Pina
Abacaxi

Mango

ARE YOUR CHILDREN SAFE IN THE SEA ?

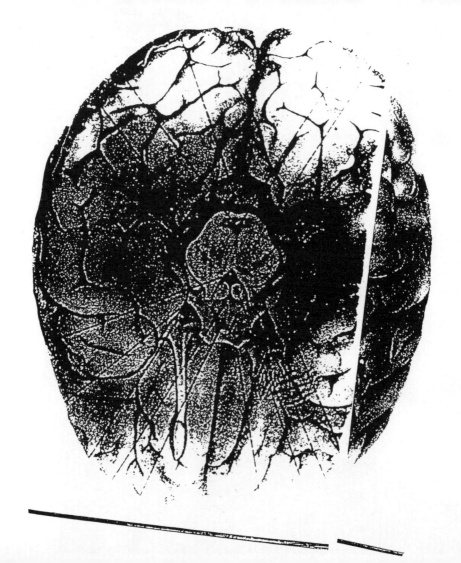

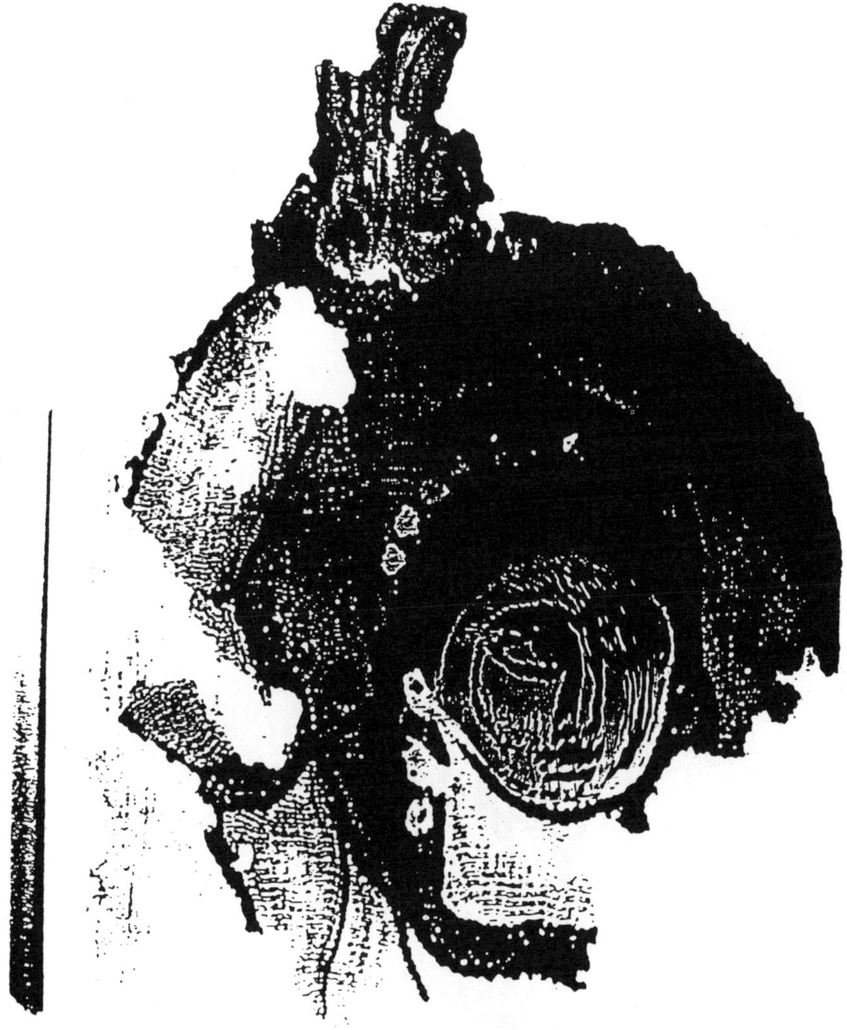

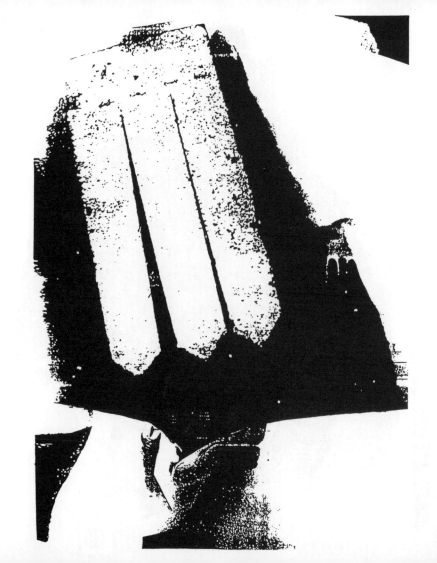

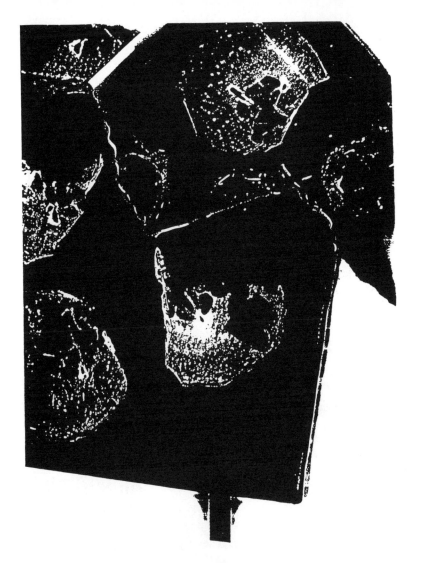

a shrewdness of apes
a sleuth of bears
a murder of crows
a dule of doves
a fesnying of ferrets
a gaggle of geese
a sounder of hogs
a smuck of jellyfish
a mob of kangeroos
a desert of lapwings
a richesse of martens
a charm of nightingales
a drove of oxen
an ostentation of peacocks
a beven of quails
an unkindness of ravens
a dopping of sheldrake
a knob of toads
a plump of waterfowl
a herd (bird?) of yaks

YARR   YAUP   YARK   YOWL   YACK

YADDER   YAH   YAFF   YAFFLE

YELP   YAPP   YAHOO   YALE

YAMMER   YABBER   YAMPH   YARKEN

YARL   YARM   YAW   YAW-HAW

YAWL   YAWLER   YAWPER   YEET

YAW-YAW   YDAD   YED   YEDDER

YE-HO   YEI   YELL   YELLOGH

YEP   YERK   YERR   YEX   YEST

YHELLE   YIKE   YIP   YIRR

YO   YOAKS   YODEL   YOICKS

YOKER   YOAK   YOLL   YOLP

YOMER   YOOP   YOLP   YOMMER

YOUDLE   YOWT   YUCKLE   YAK

YATTER   YOP   YUP   YAKALO

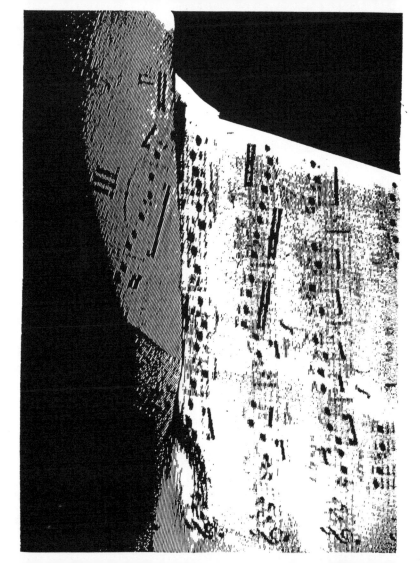

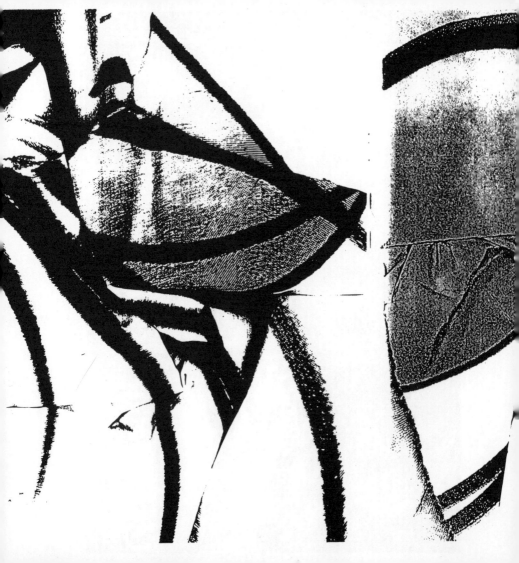

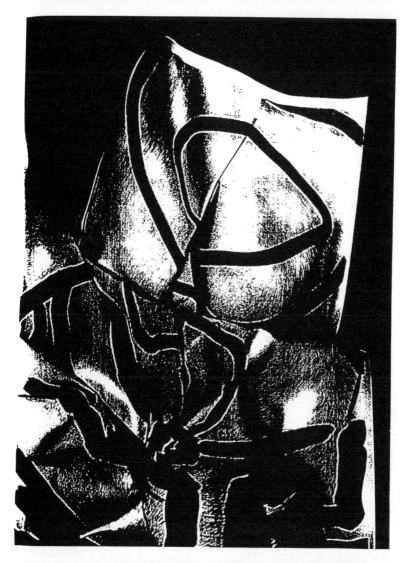

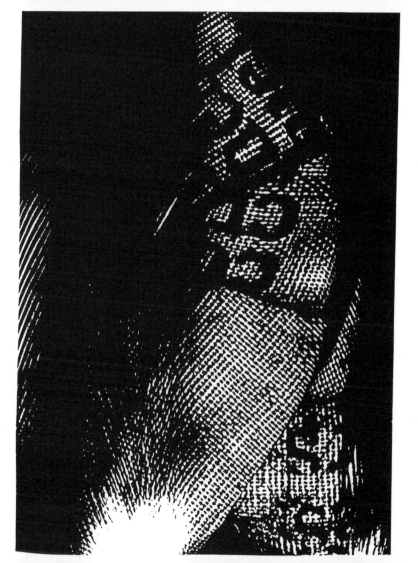

Index

* = title from the Domestic Ambient Noise series (with Lawrence Upton)

Cover from: Glossolalie un Hallali (Writers Forum 1997)